Tell me about
THINGS AT HOME

Also in this series

Tell Me About: THE EARTH AND SKY

Other titles in preparation

Tell me about THINGS AT HOME

Text by Michèle Kahn
Translated by Jane Fior

Illustrations by Michèle Trumel

COLLINS

AROUND THE HOUSE

AT THE TABLE

MY BODY AND MY CLOTHES

Around the house

● ***Where does electric light come from?***

If you've ever been in the country, you may have noticed tall wooden or concrete posts with thick wires running from them. Birds like to perch up there. They don't know that these wires carry electricity to people's homes. It is because of electricity that we can turn on the light, and the television, and all sorts of other appliances.

● ***How does electricity get to our homes?***

It always travels in electrical wiring. There is metal on the inside of this wire, and the electricity runs along it, rather like water running through a pipe. When electricity is travelling along like this, we call it the electrical current.

In our homes everything which lights up is connected to the electrical wiring, even though you can't always see it. Wiring is often hidden away inside the walls.

- ***How do the lights go on?***

Take a good look at the lamp hanging from your ceiling or standing on the table. You'll see that it has one or more glass bulbs: these are electric light bulbs. Inside each bulb there is a very small thin wire. This wire lights up when you press the switch, and the electric light becomes very bright, like a little sun.
When you switch it on, the switch allows the electrical current to go through the wire to the bulb. When you switch it off, it stops the current going through.

- ***What is an electrical appliance?***

It is an appliance which works on electricity. It has a piece of wire connected to it, and at the end of this wire there is a plug with three metal prongs. To make the machine work, the plug with its prongs has to be pushed into the holes of an electric point. Have a look around you. The vacuum cleaner, the electric mixer, the refrigerator, the television, and lots of other appliances all work on electricity.

- ***Why is it dangerous to touch an electrical appliance with wet hands?***

If you touch an electrical appliance with wet hands, the electricity can pass through the water and into your body. This is very dangerous because it can kill you. Always dry your hands properly before you touch anything electric. Take care when you turn on the light or the television. And remember that you must never play with electric plugs or points.

NO!

- ***Where does the water out of the tap come from?***

Tap water comes from a river, a spring, or from a well. First of all, it is made pure in a factory and then brought to your house in huge pipes. You can't see these pipes because they are buried underneath the road and the pavements.

- ***Can I drink water out of any tap?***

At home, you should be able to drink water out of any of the cold water taps. It has been filtered, which means cleaned, before getting to your house. But you must be careful about taps and drinking fountains that you may see in the street, on stations, or in gardens. If there is a notice saying 'Drinking Water' you can drink it. If it says 'Unsuitable for Drinking', or has no notice on at all, don't drink it! The germs in dirty water can make you very ill.

- ***How do we get hot water?***

Most homes have a water heater of some kind. In small houses and in some flats you can usually see the water heater that heats the family's water. But in big blocks of flats, there is often a very large water heater down in the cellar which heats the water for all the families living there. This is the central heating boiler.

drinking water
not for drinking

● ***Is there always water in the tap?***

You are used to getting water every time you turn on the tap. But maybe one day a plumber will come to your house to do some repairs, and the water will be cut off. There won't be any for several hours. In the summer there is sometimes a water shortage if it has been very hot and hasn't rained for a long time.

● ***Where does the water in the basin go?***

When we have used water to wash our clothes, to clean our vegetables, or to have a bath or flush the lavatory, the water becomes dirty water. Dirty water goes down under the ground through pipes, and then flows into very big pipes – the drains. The drains take the water to the sewage works, where it is cleaned. It then travels to the nearest suitable river, where it is allowed to run out.

● ***Why is there a little cloud in the air when water is boiling?***

This little cloud is called steam. When water is very hot, it rises in tiny little drops. When these little drops come out of the kettle or the saucepan, they meet the cold air outside and they begin to cool. They turn a grey-whitish colour, and you see them all gathered together in that cloud of steam.

- ***When does water turn into ice?***

When it is very cold (below 0°C on the thermometer), water freezes. In winter, you can sometimes see puddles in the street which have frozen and turned into ice.
At home you can make ice cubes by pouring water into little moulds which fit into the top of the refrigerator. Feel how cold they are!

- ***Why do we need refrigerators?***

Food keeps fresh longer when it is cold, and so a machine was invented to make coldness: the refrigerator. A refrigerator helps to keep food fresh for several days. Without it, we would have to buy meat, milk, butter and lots of other things fresh each day, and we would have to eat them straightaway.

- ***How does the refrigerator work?***

You've probably wondered why the refrigerator sometimes purrs like a great big cat. This noise comes from the electric motor which makes the refrigerator cold. If the electricity is turned off, the motor stops, and slowly all the ice melts and turns to water. Look out for the puddle on the floor!
And what about the light some people have inside their refrigerators? Is it on all the time? No. It turns off each time the door is closed, and only lights up when the door is opened again.

- ***Where are the people who talk on the radio and on the television?***

They are in a building where radio and television broadcasts are prepared. The room they work in is called a studio. They talk into a microphone or into a camera which 'takes' their picture. Then the voice and the picture are sent through the air, although you can't see them because they are invisible. By switching on your radio or television, you can see and hear them immediately.

- ***Why do people put an aerial on the roof?***

The voices and pictures for the television travel through the air. But sometimes hills, mountains, high buildings and the walls of your house get in the way. But the aerial, fixed high on the roof, helps to catch the pictures and the voices. They then come down a thick wire and into your television. Thanks to the aerial, the picture and sound are clear.

- ***What does watching the news mean?***

When people listen to the news on the radio or watch it on the television, they learn about all the important things that are happening in the world, both the good things and the bad things. Stories or events that are on the news have really happened. Some of the things you see in other programmes are not true; they are made up.

- ***Why do I have to keep things tidy?***

Imagine that you have taken all your toys out of the toy cupboard. Next, you build yourself a house using all the chairs. After that, you decide to read some books. Now you want to do some drawing — but there is no space left! And anyway, in all the mess you can't even find your crayons. You'll have to tidy everything up. If you don't, you won't be able to find anything at all. Soon there won't even be enough space for you in your room!

- ***Why do clothes have to be ironed?***

When they have been washed, your clothes become creased, like a piece of paper crushed in your hand. Sometimes you may want to wear them like that, but usually it's nicer to wear a dress or a pair of trousers that looks smooth and crisp. If a hot iron is run over creased material, all the creases disappear, and the material is flat and smooth. There are some materials that don't crease, and so they don't need any ironing.

- ***Why can't I touch everything?***

You probably want to touch everything – soft things, bright things, things that you see for the first time. "Don't touch!" say grown-ups. Why not?. Because some delicate things smash if you drop them: vases and china for example. Some appliances break if they are not used properly. And then there are the dangerous things, like the hotplate on the stove. Take care! You'll burn yourself if you touch it.

- ***What does the vacuum cleaner do?***

Sometimes you can see a fine powder over the furniture and on the floor. This is dust. Dust is always in the air and it collects underneath beds and furniture, forming little balls of fluff. The vacuum cleaner's motor sucks up the dust into a bag inside the cleaner. Later the dust is emptied into the dustbin.

- ***What happens to things that go down a rubbish chute?***

In blocks of flats, each floor usually has a rubbish chute. If you put some vegetable peelings in a plastic bag and throw them down the chute, you can hear the package tumble down inside it. Where does it go? It falls into a very large dustbin at the bottom. When the dustbin is full, the caretaker wheels it away and puts an empty one in its place.

If you live in a house, you will put your rubbish straight into your own dustbin.

- ***Where does wood come from?***

Have you got a chest of drawers made of wood in your room? Do you know its story?

It was once a tree growing in the forest. One day, it was chopped down and taken to the sawmill. There, machines were used to saw the tree into planks. Later on, a carpenter used the planks to make your chest of drawers.

At the table

- ***How is bread made?***

The baker pours a lot of flour, a little water, some salt and some yeast into a large steel bowl. Big paddles mix it all up into dough, and then the baker waits for the dough to rise. When it is ready, he cuts the dough into pieces, shapes them into loaves, and puts the loaves into a hot oven to bake. When they are ready, the loaves will be crusty and golden.

- ***Where does flour come from?***

Flour is made from finely ground wheat. Wheat is grown in fields by farmers. At the beginning of the summer, you can see huge fields of wheat growing in the country, and as it ripens, the golden ears sway in the wind. Soon, with the help of machines, the wheat is cut and gathered. The grains are taken to the flourmill and ground into flour. This flour is used to make bread, and puddings and all sorts of delicious cakes.

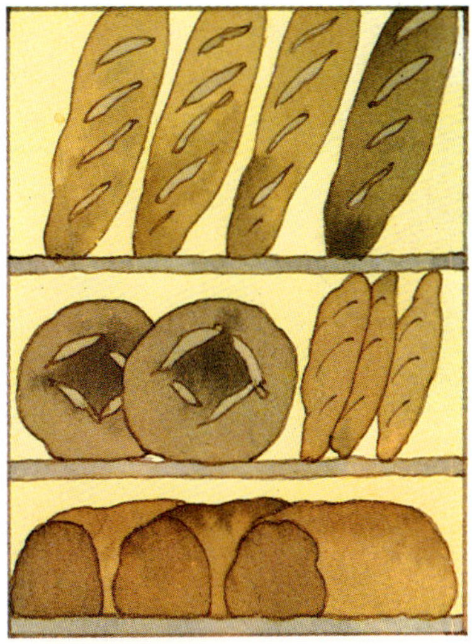

flour

• *Why do cows give us milk?*

Cows produce milk after the birth of their first calf. As soon as the calf is born, the cow will make more than enough milk to feed it. So every morning and every evening, the cows on the farm are milked, which means that milk is taken from their udders and poured into large milk churns. These are then taken to the local dairy where the milk is bottled and sold by the milkman.

• *Where does powdered milk come from?*

Powdered milk is made from the fresh milk of cows. By heating the milk to a very high temperature, you can remove all the water it contains. The milk that remains is in the form of a powder, which is easy to package and to use because it does not go sour like fresh milk.

• *Why does milk boil over sometimes?*

As the milk begins to get hot, you can see a thin skin forming on its surface. When the milk gets hotter still, it boils. Bubbles form. The bubbles want to rise, so they push up the skin and pour over the side of the saucepan. If you don't want milk to boil over, you must lower the heat as soon as the first bubble appears.

Where does butter come from?

Butter is made from fresh cows' milk. If milk is allowed to stand for a while, a layer of cream rises to the top. To make butter, the cream is separated from the milk and churned until it is solid. Before we had machines to do this work for us, butter was made in butter churns that were turned by hand. Milk is also used to make cheese, yoghourts and ice-cream.

Why does butter soften when you take it out of the refrigerator?

When butter is taken out of the refrigerator, it is quite hard. It is sometimes so hard that it is difficult to spread. The cold has caused the fat contained in the butter to harden. The warmer temperature of the room melts the fat again, and so the butter begins to soften. If you leave butter in the sun, or cook it, it becomes as liquid as oil.

Where does cocoa come from?

Cocoa trees grow in some very hot countries. They have very large fruit and each one contains up to 40 beans. When these beans are dried, roasted, peeled and ground, we get cocoa powder. We can mix this with sugar and hot milk to get hot chocolate.

- ***Where does coffee come from?***

Do you know what a shrub is? It is a little tree whose bottom branches grow so low down the trunk that they sometimes touch the ground. Coffee is a shrub which is grown in some hot countries. It has berries and each berry contains two coffee beans. The beans must be picked, dried, peeled and roasted before they can be put into packets.

- ***Why do we grind coffee?***

If you want some instant coffee, you put a spoonful in your cup, pour in hot milk or water, stir it up, and drink it. But fresh coffee is prepared quite differently. It is the taste and the smell that is so good, not the ground beans. So we grind the coffee beans and pour boiling water over them. The water slowly drips through and as it does so, the ground coffee flavours and colours the water. It is best to grind the beans at the last minute, otherwise the smell disappears and the coffee loses its taste.

- ***Where does tea come from?***

Tea is a little bush which grows in some countries where the weather is both very hot and very damp, in China and India for example. First the leaves are picked, and then they are dried. We use small pieces of leaf when we make a pot of tea. As with coffee grounds, we don't drink tea-leaves, they are left in the tea strainer.

- ***Where does sugar come from?***

Many plants contain sugar. We get most of ours from sugar beet or from sugar cane that grows in hot countries. By crushing sugar beet in very large machines, a sweet syrup is obtained. Other machines make granulated sugar, sugar lumps, and icing sugar. We use icing sugar when we make cakes and sweets.

- ***What happens to sugar when you put it in your tea?***

If you drop a lump of sugar into a cup of tea or a glass of water, it separates into very tiny pieces which stay at the bottom of the glass. Then it begins to dissolve. If you stir the water with a spoon, the sugar will disappear completely. Adding a lump of sugar to your cup of tea makes it taste sweet.

- ***Who makes honey?***

A man? A woman? A machine? None of these. It is made by an insect – a bee. Have you ever noticed a bee settling on one flower after another? It is gathering nectar. Nectar is a kind of sugar which the bee collects and stores in the form of honey in its nest or in its hive. A hive is a little house made by a beekeeper. The bees live there, and the beekeeper collects their honey.

honey
honey

- ***Why can't I just eat fruit?***

If you are very fond of fruit, perhaps you'd like to eat it all the time? How lovely it would be just to eat oranges, bananas, apricots, strawberries, nuts . . ! But your body needs other food such as meat, eggs, milk, cheese and vegetables too. If you are to grow big and strong, you will need some of these foods every day.

- ***Why do we peel fruit before we eat it?***

The skin of bananas, oranges and pineapples is very thick and gives us stomach-ache if we try to eat it. Apples, peaches and pears have thinner skin, which we can eat. However, when fruit is growing, it is often sprayed with a special chemical which keeps insects away. This chemical can make us ill. Often the fruit has had to travel a long way to get to us too, and it may be dirty. So you see, it is best to peel fruit, or if you wish to eat the skin, to wash it well before you do so.

- ***Why can't we eat cherries all the year round?***

Cherries grow on cherry trees. In the autumn, the trees begin to lose their leaves, and by winter the branches are quite bare. In spring, the sun makes them grow new leaves and flowers. At the centre of each flower is a tiny green fruit which grows into a cherry. It will take until the summer for it to be ripe and juicy, ready for us to eat. And summer comes only once a year.

• *Where does salt come from?*

If you have ever bathed in the sea, you know how salty the water is. This salt can be collected in special salt pens. Here the sea is shallow, and as the water evaporates in the sun, it leaves a fine powder behind on the ground. This is salt. The salt has to be shovelled up and left to dry. Another kind of salt is also found in the ground.

• *Where does pepper come from?*

Pepper is the fruit of the pepper plant and it grows in hot countries. Each fruit is a little black berry which we call a peppercorn. In the grocer's shop, you can buy white pepper too. This is black pepper which has been peeled and it is not so strong. At the table, we use ground pepper. You put a little on your meat or your egg to season it. But take care, only use a little pepper for it is very strong.

• *What are spices?*

Spices are plants which add taste to food and we use them in the form of powder or flakes. They often have pretty names: cinnamon, cloves, ginger, nutmeg, mustard, vanilla, paprika. Pepper is a spice too. Gingerbread tastes the way it does because we add spices to the mixture when we are making it.

GROCER

bay
clove
mustard
vanilla
cinnamon
gingerbread
nutmeg
paprika
mustard
mustard

- ***Why is water sometimes sold in bottles?***

If you look at the label on bottled water, you'll see that it is spring water. When water comes out of the ground like this, it is clean and pure. It can be collected and put into bottles for drinking. Pure spring water often tastes much nicer than tap water, and it can be used to cure people who are unwell. Not all bottled water tastes the same, and some of it is fizzy.

- ***Can I drink lemonade all the time?***

Lemonade is delicious, and so are many other fizzy drinks. Fruit juice is nice too. You probably think that they taste much better than water. However, your body needs water, plain simple water without anything added to it. Drink lemonade when you want a treat, but drink water when you are thirsty. Water quenches your thirst the best.

- ***Why must I be careful when I drink something from a bottle?***

We keep all sorts of liquids in bottles — for example, milk, fruit juice, and water. But not all liquids are for drinking. Bleach, for example, is stored in bottles and it is for cleaning. It is poisonous and could kill you if you drank it. Many other liquids are poisonous too. So unless you are absolutely sure what is in a bottle, never drink from it without first asking permission.

drinking water

● *Why must I wash my hands before I eat?*

Think of all the different things you can touch in a short space of time. Sand, dogs, cats . . .. Each time you touch something, germs get on to your hands. Germs are everywhere, and they are invisible. Some germs can make you ill if you swallow them, so it is important to wash your hands before eating anything. And if you want to wash them properly, you must use soap.

● *Can I eat with my fingers?*

Eating with your fingers or drinking soup straight from the bowl is easier and much more fun than using a knife, fork and spoon. Indeed, in some countries, people do eat in this way. But if you find yourself at the table with people who are using knives and forks, you should do the same. This is the polite thing to do. Only use your fingers when there is no risk of getting sticky.

● *Why do people say "your eyes are bigger than your stomach"?*

"Oh, look at this lovely chocolate cake! May I have a great big slice? And that delicious strawberry ice-cream, I could eat a whole plateful!" But could you really eat all that? Would your stomach have enough room for all the things your eyes have taken a fancy to? If your eyes are bigger than your stomach, you'll end up leaving good food on your plate. And that's a shame and a waste.

My body and my clothes

- ***Why does the water rise when I get into the bath?***

When you get into the bath, the water is pushed aside to make room for you. The further you get in, the more water is pushed aside and the more it rises. If you only get halfway into the bath, the water won't rise as high as it will if you let the water cover you completely. A large man makes the bathwater rise much higher than a small child.

- ***Where do sponges come from?***

Sponges were once animals that lived at the bottom of the sea. They are a strange kind of animal, aren't they? They have no eyes, no mouths, no paws; in fact, they are more like plants. The sponges we use for washing are the remains of the animals once they have been dried. Nowadays we often use man-made sponges which are made out of plastic. They come in all sorts of colours.

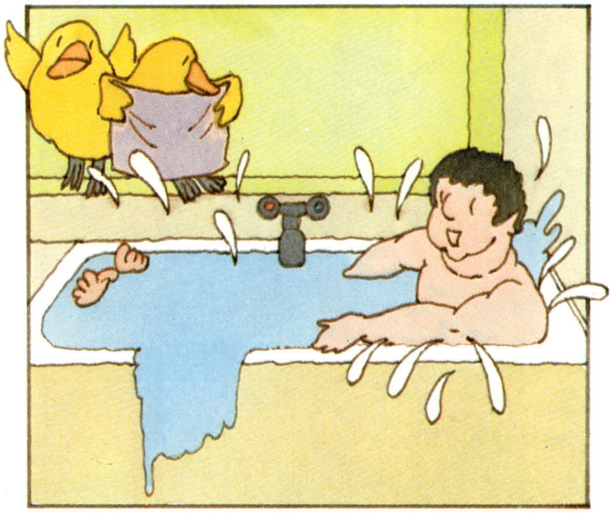

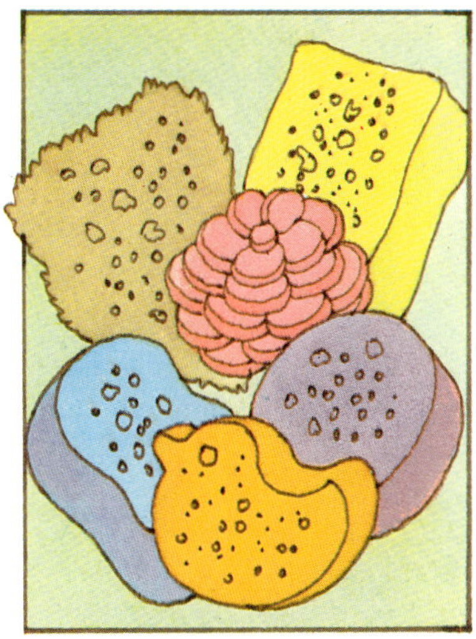

• *Why do we have to clean our teeth so often?*

When we eat something, specks of food stick to our teeth and can slowly rot them. This is particularly true of sugar and sweets. Small holes, called cavities, start to appear in our teeth, and these have to be filled by a dentist. If not, the holes will get bigger and bigger and damage the whole tooth, which may have to be taken out. If we brush our teeth morning and night, this won't happen.

• *Why does everyone have to have their own toothbrush?*

Our mouths are full of germs, although we neither see them nor feel them. These small living things can carry disease. For example, you might have in your mouth the germs which cause tonsillitis even though you feel perfectly well. If you let your little brother use your toothbrush, he could catch tonsillitis from you.

• *Why do children lose their teeth?*

Your baby teeth, which are called milk teeth, are just the right size for your jaw. As you get bigger, your jaw gets bigger too, and it needs bigger teeth to fit it. Inside your gums, hidden underneath your milk teeth, bigger, stronger teeth are waiting. These are your grown-up teeth. They gently push on your milk teeth so that finally these drop out. This does not hurt at all.

- ***Why do people put cream on their faces?***

Skin is delicate, and there are a great many things that can damage it: wind, cold weather, sun, sometimes even soap. It feels rough when you touch it. But if you smoothe on a little cream, it will feel soft again. Cream can also be put on skin to protect it — for example, suncream stops our skin becoming burnt and red in the sun.

- ***What is soap for?***

If you have a shower, most of the dust and dirt on your body will be washed away; however, really grimy marks won't come off. Water alone can't wash butter from your fingers, for example, only soap can wash away the oil in the butter and any other oil which is on your skin. Soap has another important job; it helps fight germs.

- ***Why do we have to comb our hair?***

If you don't comb your hair at all, you'll end up looking like a hedgehog. That might be fun, but it is not good for your hair. It will get so tangled that it will be impossible to comb it. The only way to remove the tangles will be to cut them out. Brushing and combing your hair properly is the only way to keep it in good condition.

- ***Why do things hurt?***

Our skin is sensitive, which means that it can feel if something is cold, or soft, or hot, or if something hurts. Pain is a warning that something dangerous is happening. If we cut ourselves, for example, the pain makes us inspect the wound. If it is bleeding, we must clean it and cover it quickly to make sure that dangerous germs do not get into the cut. If we burn our finger, the pain is so strong that we quickly pull our finger away from the heat. Without the pain, we might leave our finger to burn. It is a good thing that we can feel pain!

- ***Why do we put disinfectant on cuts?***

Imagine that you have fallen over and cut your knee. "Quick," says your mother, "I'll just put on a little disinfectant." Don't worry, it won't hurt. The disinfectant will help to clean the wound and will kill any germs that may be in it. Thanks to the disinfectant, your knee won't get infected and will soon be better.

- ***Why do people get ill?***

Your body is like a musical instrument made up of a great many different parts. Sometimes it doesn't sound right. One of the parts has broken, or the instrument is out of tune. When you feel unwell, it is because one of your parts is damaged, or perhaps because some invisible germ has got into your body. The doctor will examine you to see how best to cure you.

- ***Why do we have a thermometer?***

A thermometer can be used to measure the temperature of your body. By looking at it, it is possible to see whether your body is too hot or too cold. When you are well, the thermometer will show about 37°C. If the silver line of the mercury goes above this point, it means that you have a temperature, and so we know that you are ill. You probably won't be feeling very well. You may feel too hot or too cold or sometimes even both.

- ***Can my friends visit me when I am ill?***

It can be very boring, lying in bed all alone. If only some friends would come round for a visit! Unfortunately this isn't always possible. Some illnesses are contagious. This means that your friends might catch your illness if they come to see you. Grown-ups have to come close to you in order to look after you, but they don't usually catch children's diseases.

- ***Why do we take medicine?***

Quite simply, to help us to get well. The pink pills, the white powder, the green syrup all go down inside you and enter your blood. Your blood then carries the medicine to the part of your body which needs help to get better. But take care! Never take any pill or other kind of medicine unless a grown-up tells you to. If you took the wrong medicine by mistake, you could make yourself very ill indeed.

39°5
39°
38°5
38°
37°5
37°

- ***Why do people wear clothes?***

In cold countries people wear thick warm clothes, often leaving only their faces uncovered. In very hot countries there are people who wear hardly any clothes at all, though others cover themselves from head to foot in order to protect themselves from the sun. We choose our clothes to please ourselves and to suit the weather.

- ***Where does the wool of my pullover come from?***

Have you noticed how sheep are covered with curly wool? Every spring, the wool is cut off with big shears or with an electric machine and then it is spun. That means that it is made into one long thread. The natural colour of wool is usually off-white, but it can be dyed all sorts of colours. Now it is ready for knitting.

- ***Where does the cotton of my tee-shirt come from?***

In some hot countries, cotton plants are grown. They have white flowers that become fruit. This fruit is about the size of a nut and when it is ripe, a sort of fluff appears. This fluff is cotton. First of all, it has to be picked and cleaned, and then it can either be made into cotton wool or it can be spun. After spinning, the thread is fed into a loom which weaves it into material.

- ***What is leather?***

Your shoes are probably made of leather, which comes from the skin of an animal. In order to make leather, the skin has to be prepared and then dyed. We only get leather from certain animals. You won't find shoes made of chicken leather! It has to be a thick skin like that of oxen, calves, cows, sheep, pigs or even crocodiles. Crocodile skin is very rare and you can recognize it by its scaly surface.

- ***What is nylon?***

Nylon brushes, nylon tights, nylon tablecloths: nylon is everywhere. It is called a man-made material because it isn't formed naturally. It is made in a factory. To make nylon, oil and coal are mixed with various other products. The result is a tank of foamy paste which is pulled out in strings like chewing gum in order to make the thread.

- ***Where does fur come from?***

Have you seen people wearing fur jackets or fur caps in winter when it is cold? Just like leather, fur is the skin of an animal, but it still has its hair. Certain species of animals have become rare because men have killed them for their skins, and so scientists have invented ways of imitating fur with man-made materials. Now it is possible to have fur made of nylon!

● What can I use for dressing-up?

If you want to dress up as a bride or a ghost, the curtains seem just the thing! But don't forget to ask your mother or your father if they'll allow you to take them down. Someone has probably taken a long time to wash and iron them. Most likely you'll be given an old curtain or a sheet to play with instead. Then it won't matter if it gets dirty or torn.

● Can I paint my face?

It's fun to turn yourself into a Red Indian or a circus clown! But be careful! Some paints can give you horrid spots or make marks on your skin that are difficult to remove. Don't use any paint unless you are sure that it is suitable. Your mother may prefer to lend you some of her make-up.

● Why must I never put my head inside a plastic bag?

Suppose you see a plastic bag lying about in your room. You think maybe you'll try hiding inside it by putting it over your head. Never do that! Plastic does not allow air to pass through it. If you can't get air, you suffocate, and so unless the plastic bag is removed immediately, it could be very dangerous. Some children have died because they have played with plastic bags.

NO!
YES
but not for long

- ***Why do we go to bed at night?***

At the end of the day your body is tired. You want to close your eyes, and that means that you need rest. After a night's sleep you'll be ready to run and jump, work, laugh and play. We could sleep in the day and stay awake at night, but it is much better to be awake in the daylight.

- ***Why do we wear pyjamas or nightdresses?***

Our day clothes get dirty so it is nicer to sleep in clothes that are only worn at home. We also sleep best when we are completely comfortable, so we don't want our nightclothes to be made of scratchy material or to have tight elastic or fastenings. Instead, they are designed to be loose and are made in soft materials.

- ***Why do we close our eyes when we go to sleep?***

Try lifting a very heavy sack. The muscles of your arm will harden in two places. The muscles in your body help you to stand up and move about. When you lie down quietly they no longer have to work, and when you go to sleep they can relax completely. The little muscles that keep your eyelids open relax too, so very gently they close.

- ***Why do people snore?***

You've probably heard grown-ups snoring in their sleep. It makes a funny noise. Did you know that you snore sometimes too? When you have a cold and your nose is stopped up, you breathe with your mouth open instead of using your nose. If you are lying on your back, this kind of breathing can be very noisy. Some people always breathe through their mouths when they are asleep, even when they haven't got a cold.

- ***What is a nightmare?***

A nightmare is a frightening dream in which horrid things happen to you. People sometimes have nightmares when they are afraid of something. Sometimes it is because they have a temperature or have eaten too much. Whatever the reason, it's nice to be able to wake up and say "Thank goodness, it was just a nightmare!"

- ***Are dreams real?***

Suppose last night you dreamed of flowers as tall as trees. They aren't real, of course, because there aren't such things. But maybe you are so fond of flowers that in your dream you made them very important. Or perhaps you'd like to be really little, small enough to hide underneath flowers. Nice dreams can help us understand what we want, but they don't necessarily show us things that are real. So sleep well!

rrrrr rrr
rrrr
Sssh!
RRRR
RRR
RRR
R

First published in the UK in 1982 by
William Collins Sons & Co Ltd

ISBN 0 00 195832 1
Printed in Great Britain by William Collins
Sons & Co Ltd Glasgow

...duction

Ryton Organic Gardens, which is ... headquarters of HDRA – the orga... organisation, was created in 1985 out of a 22 acre green-field site. Prior to that it had been used for stabling horses and as a riding school, with the land divided into three large paddocks. Like much of Warwickshire, it had originally been bounded by mature elms, all of which succumbed to Dutch Elm Disease in the late 1970s. When HDRA took over in the winter of 1985, only a handful of mature oaks remained - everything else has been planted since.

Our aim at Ryton is to be a showcase for organic gardening. When we began, many people still believed that without chemical fertilisers and pesticides, it was impossible to garden successfully. Attitudes to organic growing have changed out of all recognition in the intervening years, but many people still have a partial understanding of the practicalities. That probably explains why the composting demonstration is our most popular display.

In September 2002 we embarked on a major transformation of the gardens, creating a new visitor centre – The Vegetable Kingdom. As well as our exciting new indoor exhibition,

...everal new gardens ...ork of garden paths, making the grounds accessible for all throughout the year.

We hope that you enjoy your visit to Ryton and that, if you don't already garden organically, you might put it into practice in your own garden. Recycling garden waste instead of throwing it away, encouraging wildlife, and minimising chemical pollution, are an integral part of the organic approach. It makes such good sense as society as a whole strives to become more sustainable in the 21st century.

Alan and Jackie Gear
Directors, HDRA.
June 2003

We gratefully acknowledge the support of Link-a-Bord in sponsoring this publication. Link-a-Bord is a manufacturer of modular, recycled plastic compost bins & containers.

The Vegetable Kingdom

For thirty years HDRA has been campaigning to save Britain's traditional vegetable varieties, which are threatened by a combination of commercial pressures and red tape.

Most of us get our vegetables from supermarkets where what counts most is regularity of shape and colour, plus a flawless appearance. These are not qualities that would have carried much weight with earlier generations, when most people either grew vegetables at home, or bought from the local market. Flavour, continuity of picking and delicate skins were what mattered to them.

As an example, the Victorians grew over 120 different varieties of tall garden pea providing a continuous picking of freshly shelled peas throughout the summer months. A century later, frozen peas reign supreme. Today's food processors require varieties where all the peas ripen at once. Added to this, a series of EU regulations

If space is at a premium, why not grow vegetables in containers?

from the mid 1970s onwards makes the sale of vegetable seeds a criminal offence unless the variety is registered on a National or EU list. Although exemptions were made for some older varieties, many slipped through the net. With the cost of registration running into thousands of pounds a time, the future for hundreds of historic varieties looked bleak.

To keep these older varieties alive, in 1975 HDRA created **the Heritage Seed Library** (HSL). Instead of selling seeds, we gave them away! Today over 800 different kinds are kept at Ryton, and are grown and enjoyed by more than 10,000 HSL members (see page 31). Included are several late 19th century tall peas, including Champion of England and the incomparable Ne Plus Ultra, which we have rescued from extinction.

These varieties are kept in **The Vegetable Kingdom** – a specially designed building erected in 2003. Here seeds are carefully kept under controlled chilled and deep frozen conditions for long term storage, as well as being cleaned and packeted for use by Heritage Seed Library members.

But there is a broader educational purpose to The Vegetable Kingdom. Britain has a wonderful heritage of vegetable varieties that has grown and evolved over the centuries. Successive waves of visitors, immigrants and returning explorers have brought vegetable seeds with them. The Romans introduced lettuce and garlic, for example; in the 9th century, Arabs and Jews brought cauliflowers and aubergines, whilst the exploration of the New World by

Columbus paved the way for the arrival of tomatoes, potatoes and runner beans. This continues to the present day with Afro Caribbean and Asian immigrants bringing with them vegetables, such as kalaloo, that they would have grown back home.

The role of The Vegetable Kingdom is to highlight this aspect of Britain's heritage, and to show how important vegetables are to our health and well-being. Despite being constantly urged by Government to eat five fruit and vegetables a day, few do, whilst for many people their entire vegetable intake consists of just chips and baked beans.

Our displays in The Vegetable Kingdom, involving models, graphics, interactive and computer games, are intended to inform and be fun, to be interesting and entertaining for all, but especially for children.

The Building

We have taken great care to use recycled materials and incorporate conservation features wherever possible, such as the striking living sedum roof. The demonstration exhibits are made from environmentally friendly papier maché in preference to glass fibre resin; the hedges from wool, and the carcassing from a new type of MDF that avoids the use of toxic chemicals.

For further information about vegetables HDRA's booklet 'Vegetables – A Concise Guide' is available in the shop.

1 Vegetable Inspirations

This garden, which we have called **Vegetable Inspirations** is the first one you enter from the building. The formal layout is designed to provide a stage on which the vegetables star, showing off their good looks as objects of garden interest as well as being edible.

The beds immediately facing you, with the decorative metal fencing, are planted with a mixture of perennial ornamentals. Studded amongst them you will also find some vegetables, chosen principally for their colour.

Beyond these you reach a reflective pond flanked by two Alitex cold frames and, behind them, matching vegetable beds. Each year we will feature a different group of related crops in these beds. The obelisks in the centre of these beds are made of Welsh upland larch, which has good natural durability.

Note the carved stainless steel panels in the fence in front of you. These were created by the artist Simon Packard, who also designed the elaborate Vegetable Kingdom archway in steel viewed earlier. Beyond, the fencing around the plant sales area is made from a product called Knotwood, made mainly of recycled plastic. The Vegetable Inspirations garden as a whole was designed by landscape architects, LandArt.

Once you have enjoyed this garden to the full, head towards the corner of the building where you will find the entrance to the **Vegetable Way**.

A list of the plants in this garden is available from the shop counter.

Vegetable Way 2

In this garden we combine many practical ideas for growing vegetables organically. The first of the two displays on your right illustrates *growing in beds*. The main advantage of bed gardening is that you can space crops more closely together. Beds here are 1.2m (4ft) wide, just enough to reach the middle from the paths.

Digging is physically arduous and not everyone either wants to, or can, do it. Hence the *no-dig garden*. The soil is cultivated only shallowly, whilst crops such as potatoes are grown close to the surface and covered with a very heavy mulch to exclude light. When it's supper time, lift the mulch and select your spuds!

Now follow the path to the left with a flower border on your right. Here we are showing *unusual vegetables*. We have selected some less common varieties and sorts of vegetables for you to try in your garden. Apart from providing a little chic in the kitchen, these vegetables can sometimes be less trouble to grow as, being uncommon, they have fewer pests.

Next, turn left in front of the glasshouse, go under the grape arches to the left, then into the *courtyard garden* on the right.

Even if your garden is tiny, you can grow some salads and vegetables to pick fresh. In this space you will find a small greenhouse, vegetables in containers and climbing vegetables, such as beans, growing in the borders. The 'square foot' garden plot in here shows a curious but effective way to maximise use of a small area of soil with minimal labour.

Return to the superb *Alitex glasshouse*. This houses winter and summer crops, allowing us to harvest something almost all year round. In winter you will see winter purslane, mizuna, mibuna and other oriental greens, endive, chicory and various salads. In summer we will be growing a range of heat-loving plants, some of them quite unusual. Between the seasons we will aim for early and late crops, helped on by the protection of the glass.

On the other side of the glasshouse there is a display of HSL varieties, bordered by a low hedge of *Ilex crenata*, which looks very similar to dwarf box.

Natural materials, chosen with care for the environment, have been used throughout.

The Heritage Seed Library is now recognised as one of Europe's most effective seed conservation and distribution schemes. In this area you can see some of these rare gems and demonstrations of practical seed saving.

Turn left and follow the path back towards the building. On your right hand side is an ornamental border in which *flowers and vegetables* happily intermingle. If you do not want a full-sized vegetable plot but still fancy harvesting some fresh vegetables from the garden, why not grow them as part of your borders, amongst the flowers? This idea was popularised by the late Geoff Hamilton on BBC TV's *Gardener's World* programme. You will need to set aside gaps of regular size along the length to ensure a good rotation of crops. You may also want to co-ordinate your choices to the colour scheme for a visual feast as well as a culinary one.

Rainwater is collected from the roof of The Vegetable Kingdom building having been first cleaned by filters, then stored in a large underground tank, capable of holding 10,000 litres of water. When water is needed, it is pumped from this tank through additional filters and an ultra-violet sterilisation unit. If the tank runs out of water, the system automatically reverts to using mains water, so our plants need never go thirsty.

Step back into The Vegetable Kingdom where the exhibition concludes with information about cooking and eating vegetables, and there is a delightful children's play kitchen. From here you emerge back into the entrance hall and pass through the shop on your way to the rest of the gardens.

Already a great favourite with toddlers – the play kitchen.

Herb Garden 3

After leaving the shop you pass under a pergola on your way to the **Herb Garden**. Constructed in 2003, the pergola is made from green oak and has been planted up with a range of flowering climbers, including *Vitis vinifera purpurea*, *Wisteria sinensis* 'Caroline' and *Clematis Montana* 'Grandiflora'.

This extensive display of herbs spans both sides of the main path, but those on the right hand side were first planted in 1986 whereas those to the left date from 1997.

The 'old ' herb garden, flanked by a box hedge, contains over 250 plants, the majority of which are perennials requiring little maintenance. They all have their special uses, whether in cooking, medicinally, for perfumes, as dyes, fibres or just in decoration. Some have, or had, religious or spiritual significance.

Look for some more unusual plants: liquorice, variegated horseradish, English mace, buckshorn plantain, epazote and madder are all growing here.

Over in the 'new' garden are several collections of plants, including a collection of comfreys (*Symphytum*), and sea hollies (*Eryngium*). We have also extended our collection of thymes. The two perimeter beds contain medicinal herbs from China and North America, including rarely seen plants, such as poke weed, Mormon tea, blue cohosh and Cherokee mountain mint. The extra warmth offered by the glasshouse makes it possible to grow a selection of more delicate, exotic plants. In summer the senses are assaulted by a varied display of aromatic plants – basils, scented pelargoniums and tender lavenders.

These herbs are not just tasty and nutricious but are beautiful too!

A good selection of organic herbs can be bought in the shop.

4 *Pest and Disease Control Display*

The bran scattered around these lettuces acts as a deterrent to slugs.

Continue along the brick paved path until you reach a garden bounded by a holly and beech hedge. Turn up the path alongside it, with the hedge on your right until, after twenty or thirty yards, you come to the **Pest and Disease Control Display**.

All the gardens here at Ryton rely entirely on organic methods to produce healthy plants. In this display you can see examples of the pest and disease control methods we use. Prevention is just as important as control, as is providing plants with the best possible growing conditions. Ensuring that plants never go short of water or food, and that they are growing in the right location gives them the best chance of surviving attack by pests and diseases.

Convolvulus tricolor is an excellent hoverfly attractant plant

Attracting Wildlife

Encouraging 'garden friends' helps create a balance between pests and their natural enemies. Particular flowers, especially members of the daisy and carrot families, provide food for beneficial insects. Shrubby plants provide shelter throughout the year. Structures such as bird, bat and hedgehog boxes encourage these helpful creatures to take up residence in the garden.

Here are some plants that attract beneficial insects:

ANNUALS

- *Annual convolvulus, baby blue eyes, buckwheat, Californian poppy, poached egg plant (see below), mustard and Phacelia tanacetifolia*

PERENNIALS

- *Clover, fennel, golden rod, hazel, nettles, sea holly, teasel and willow*

Soil Conditions

Altering the soil conditions is a good way of controlling some diseases. Clubroot, a serious disease affecting members of the cabbage family, is discouraged by adding lime to the soil. Scab on potatoes can be prevented by adding grass mowings at planting time.

Rotation

Rotation is an important part of keeping crops healthy. Growing related plants in a different part of the garden each season helps prevent the build up of soil-borne pests and diseases. A crop rotation can last for as many years as you like – three to four is a minimum.

Resistant Varieties

Varieties of fruit, flowers and vegetables can be found that are less susceptible to particular pests and disease. Growing these is a great help in avoiding problems.

Biological Control

Biological control is a way of controlling pests by deliberately introducing beneficial insects and other creatures which eat pests. Common problems such as whitefly, red spider mite and aphids can be kept under control in the greenhouse by using particular predators or parasites that attack them.

Barriers and Traps

There are many ingenious barriers, traps and deterrents that can be helpful to the organic gardener. Some are simple, home-made devices; other are more elaborate, commercial products.

- **Bottle cloches:** remove the base of a clear plastic bottle to protect young plants against wind, frost and slugs
- **Human hair clippings:** used as a mulch around young plants have been helpful in deterring rabbits on this site
- **Roof tiles:** placed on the soil these provide shelter for slugs. Inspect and remove the slugs frequently, leaving any beetles in place
- **Buzz line:** when stretched tightly, this tape vibrates and produces a humming sound to discourage birds

- **Mesh and fleece:** (above) materials for covering plants that allow water through yet keep out flying insects; they also give some frost protection
- **Net:** protects plants from birds and butterflies

For more information on pest and disease control, there is a selection of HDRA literature and useful products available in the shop.

5 Composting Display

Making compost is at the heart of organic gardening. The **Composting Display** shows how you can turn 'muck' into 'magic' by recycling items often thought of as waste into useful resources.

Composting is part of the process of decomposition that goes on all around us, all the time, in the natural world. Anything that once lived can be broken down by various creatures that live within the soil. By providing these decomposers with ideal conditions in a compost heap, organic gardeners aim to speed up this natural process and achieve a more consistent end product.

Ideally, the end result should be a fine, dark, crumbly material with a pleasant 'earthy' smell. This contains essential plant nutrients that are released slowly when added to the soil. Compost helps to hold moisture in the soil by acting like a 'sponge'; it also improves drainage by changing the soil structure, enabling tiny soil particles to cling together in groups.

Compost bins

The most basic home-made compost bin is quite simply a cover to keep the rain out and the warmth in. A more sophisticated option is a post and wire construction lined with old carpet or cardboard. Also on display are examples of other types of compost bins that you can buy, most of which are made of plastic.

There is a wide range of compost containers on display.

Tumblers A compost tumbler is a closed container, mounted on a framework which enables it to be rotated daily. The tumbling action keeps the contents thoroughly mixed and aerated, speeding up the composting process dramatically.

Compost trench In the winter you will see a shallow trench, filled gradually over the months with kitchen waste from our restaurant. Covered over with soil to discourage vermin, the vegetable waste rots down slowly, then provides ideal growing conditions for runner beans the following summer.

Lifting the lid on Ryton's worm compost bin!

Worm composting This method of composting uses a special type of worm to convert waste material into compost. It is especially good for recycling kitchen waste and can survive on small amounts at a time. The worms need a warm, moist environment to thrive. They cannot tolerate extremes of temperature, waterlogged or acid conditions.

Leaf mould Leaves from deciduous trees break down to make an excellent soil conditioner after one year, or an ingredient for home-made potting mixtures after two.

Green manures A green manure is a crop grown primarily to benefit the soil. Here you can see examples of suitable plants, all of which are dug into the soil before they become tough or woody.

Liquid feeds Liquid feeds provide nutrients quickly for plants that are grown in pots, tubs, baskets or other restricted areas. Home-made examples are liquid manure, and nettle or comfrey 'tea'.

A good selection of compost bins can be bought in our shop.

What can you safely put in your compost bin? One of the practical exhibits that makes the composting display so popular with visitors.

6 World's Biggest Flowerpot

Leave the compost display where you entered and turn right in the direction of the **'World's Biggest Flowerpot'**, (confirmed by *The Guinness Book of Records)*. It was made by Peter Start, a Warwickshire sculptor. Measuring 2m (7ft) high with a rim circumference of 5m (16ft), it can hold a small border's-worth of flowers, and weighs over one and a half tonnes.

Nearby is a grassy area, bounded by shrubs on either side. These used to be long shrub borders that originally stretched as far as the Conservation Area. However, with the creation of The Vegetable Kingdom, they have been incorporated into the new landscaping.

Those shrubs that remain, and the new ones that have been planted, have been chosen to provide all year interest and easy maintenance. Organic methods are not just suitable for the vegetable garden; here you can see the splendid results of using them for ornamentals too. The new plantings include shrubs and perennials to cover a long season of interest. In the beds you will find, for example, amongst many other plants, *Viburnum x bodnantense* 'Deben', *Exochorda macrantha* 'The Bride', *Cotinus Coggygria* cvs, *Potentilla fruticosa* 'Abbottswood', *Rosa rugosa* cvs and *Hibiscus syriacus* cvs.

The 'Pictorial Meadow Mix' surrounding the giant pot is available from our mail order catalogue.

Top Fruit Gardens 7

Behind the giant flowerpot lies our **Top Fruit Gardens**. This area demonstrates all aspects of organic top fruit cultivation with the emphasis on apples, pears and plums.

Most of the fruit trees were planted in 1986-88. Now that they have had a chance to become established, they have started to produce a good harvest. Apples and pears give the best crops; plums are a less reliable crop on this site as they flower earlier and are therefore more prone to frost damage. A quince, a medlar and cherry trees complete the range.

Many old and rarely-grown varieties are on display here alongside more modern types. Some of these have good resistance to common diseases. Also shown are many different training and pruning systems. Trees are grown on different rootstocks, which enable visitors to see the effect this has on the final height of a tree.

Look for more unusual varieties of apples grown here:

- *Upton Pyne* • *King of the Pippins*
- *Court Pendu Plat*
- *Rev. W. Wilks* • *King Edward VII*

Now most of the trees are established they do not require regular additional feeding. Manure is occasionally added in the late spring, when needed, and covered with a hay or straw mulch to control weeds. The mulch is removed in winter.

A surface irrigation system was installed when planting. This is used every summer to ensure the trees never run short of moisture.

Wind is one of the worst enemies of fruit, and a particular problem on this formerly open site. The windbreak to the north east of the fruit area is planted with Italian alder, a common shelter belt species for orchards. Look out for the 'fedges', which are living willow, fence-like hedges.

'Wild' areas of tussocky grass have been allowed to develop here, into which a mixture of hardy perennials has been planted. This aids pest control by providing habitat for beneficial insects.

Beyond the top fruit collection is a mixed planting of trees, bushes and herbaceous plants, many of them edible, which was planted in 1994.

8 Soft Fruit Garden

The circular structure made from fence panels encloses our beautiful **Soft Fruit Garden**.

The circular wooden stockade fence provides very necessary protection against winter winds and spring frosts. In early summer, the entire structure is covered over with a huge net: this keeps out the birds, which would be all too glad to help with the fruit harvest! The net is removed in autumn to allow the birds back in. They perform a useful service by pecking over exposed soil for grubs of over-wintering pests. Another form of pest control is provided by the patches of flowers, which attract beneficial insects.

The raspberries in the centre of the circle are varieties selected to give a successive harvest through the season, including two autumn fruiting varieties. Notice the small beds on each of them. One grows strawberries, whilst the other grows flowers. These beds are rotated every three years. In the border along the fence, arctic raspberries can be found growing at the feet of the blackberry at the far end. These mat-forming diminutive raspberries fruit in July and August and die back in winter to a dormant crown.

The beds to the right contain gooseberries, whitecurrants and redcurrants of mixed varieties. These types of fruit are all suitable for training against a fence or wall. Here you can see examples of fans and cordons. The beds on the other side grow blackcurrants, Worcesterberries and jostaberries. These are all pruned as bushes. Blackcurrants are not suited to wall training owing to their habit of growth.

As well as blackberries, the rest of the fence supports climbing hybrid berries, many of which produce fruit later in the season. Look out for loganberry, tayberry, marionberry and sylvanberry.

Amelanchiers 9

The path from the soft fruit garden leads to the Bee Garden, passing a small collection of **Amelanchiers**, planted in late 2002. This genus of small trees, or hardy shrubs, is more commonly known as Juneberry, or 'snowy mespilus' on account of the spectacular white flowers which open in spring before the leaves appear, and the early ripening, purplish-black berries. *Amelanchier canadensis*, from Canada, growing to 6m, is the best known species but we have another five types here. An ideal small tree for the garden.

10 Bee Garden

The **Bee Garden** takes the shape of a hexagon, which echoes the cells of a honeycomb. Bees are valued for their ability to produce honey, but also have an essential part to play in the garden as pollinators for fruit and vegetable crops.

All the flowers here are attractive to bees by providing either pollen or nectar or sometimes both. Especially important to bees are those plants that flower early or late in the season, when the majority of plants are not in flower. Many of the plants here have other uses too; look out for the shrubby aromatic herbs and many members of the mint family.

Bees in Britain are adapted to feed on native plants but will also happily feed on many of the exotic flowers grown in gardens. Single flowered cultivars are more useful than highly bred double flowers, which provide little or no nectar.

The small structure in the centre of the garden is home to an observation hive in the summer months only. Open the door carefully to see the bees in action. The queen bee is larger than the rest and marked with a spot on her back. The garden is also visited by bees from the hives in the apiary in the far corner of the gardens, honey from which is harvested for sale in the shop. Because poisonous sprays are not used at Ryton, bees thrive here.

Rabbits are a big problem at Ryton and this garden, like all the others, is individually fenced to reduce their depredations.

Some favourite bee plants in this garden:

- *Alyssum*
- *apple*
- *blackberry*
- *crimson clover*
- *heather*
- *mustard*
- *Phacelia tanacetifolia*
- *rosebay willowherb*

Ryton Organic Gardens honey is available in the shop.

Visitors are welcome in the award winning restaurant, where freshly prepared food, made from finest organic vegetables, is available daily.

Key

- 0 The Vegetable Kingdom
- 1 Vegetable Inspirations
- 2 Vegetable Way
- 3 Herb Garden
- 4 Pest and Disease Control Display
- 5 Composting Display
- 6 World's Biggest Flowerpot
- 7 Top Fruit Gardens
- 8 Soft Fruit Garden
- 9 Amelanchiers
- 10 Bee Garden
- 11 Allotment
- 12 Stonemarket Cottage Garden
- 13 Weed Control Display
- 14 'All Muck & Magic?' TV Garden
- 15 Paradise Garden
- 16 Ryton Garden
- 17 Conservation Area
- 18 Reedbed Sewage System
- 19 Craftsman's Trees
- 20 Woodland Walk
- 21 RSPB Wildlife Garden
- 22 Rose Garden
- 23 Sun Clock
- 24 Mount
- 25 Flowers for Pleasure
- 26 Diversity in Landscape
- 27 Cook's Garden
- 28 Thrive Ryton Gardens Project
- 29 Memorial Garden
- 30 Children's Garden
- T Toilets

11 *Allotment*

The next garden you come to is the somewhat irregularly shaped **Allotment**. Growing your own vegetables saves money, and is a healthy activity, especially if you grow organically, as here.

The garden shows a large range of crops laid out to a clear, four-course rotation plan. Vegetables are grouped together into four sections, according to plant family and soil requirements. It is four years before each group returns to the same piece of ground. The sequence used is cabbage family, followed by root crops, followed by potatoes, followed by peas, beans and members of the onion family.
At the far end a large wooden bin recycles all the waste produced here into compost, and stores animal manure. The bin itself is a 'recycled' bulk potato crate.Wherever possible we have re-used materials rather than purchasing new.

The key to successful growing is to improve soil fertility so, as well as making compost, leaves are collected for leaf mould. A bed of comfrey has been planted to provide material for liquid feed, mulch and use as an activator in the compost heap.

In winter a trench is filled with kitchen waste from the restaurant, then covered over with soil, providing ideal growing conditions for the runner beans, which are planted here the following spring.

Flowers are included for their decorative value, both fresh and dried. They are also attractive to beneficial insects, which help with pest control. You can usually see some of the other pest and disease control methods mentioned earlier being put to use in this garden.

A polystyrene crate makes a useful plant container.

Not often grown, kale is a reliable winter crop.

Crimson flowered broad beans are attractive and tasty!

This garden has been created as part of HDRA's 'Organic Food for All' campaign, sponsored by Kettle Organics.

Stonemarket Cottage Garden 12

Next to the allotment is an area of grass earmarked for the **Stonemarket Cottage Garden**, which is to be built during 2003. A little further on, to the right of the path, is a small **Weed Control display**.

Butterfly attractant plants are grown wherever possible.

13 Weed Control Display

Organic gardeners do not use chemical weed killing sprays. Here you see some of the alternatives: mulches, both synthetic and natural; cultivation techniques; and mechanical methods.

Other organic methods of weed control that are not illustrated include hand weeding and hoeing. Weeds growing in gravel and other hard-standing areas are killed off by flame weeding.

'All Muck and Magic?' 14

Next door is the **'All Muck and Magic?' TV Garden**. This was created in 1989 during the second series of the popular Channel 4 organic gardening programme, much of which was filmed at Ryton.

Despite its small size, this garden shows that it is possible to grow flowers, fruit, herbs and vegetables successfully using organic methods, and still have room for a mini-pond, the essential compost heap, and space to sit and enjoy it all!

The trellis is used to support cordon apple trees, and also decorative climbers. Herbs sprawl happily over the dry, paved area, as well as thriving in pots. Vegetables are chosen for their ability to be compact and productive – no chance of finding space-hungry potatoes here.

The lean-to greenhouse enables a crop of delicious tomatoes to ripen in summer, and protects salads crops over winter.

15 *Paradise Garden*

The late Geoff Hamilton was much loved and watched by millions each week on *BBC Gardeners' World*. **The Paradise Garden** is our tribute to a great gardener and valued friend of HDRA.

There are two parts to the display, each representing a different style of Paradise Garden, the theme of Geoff's last series on television. You enter a town garden, quite formal in style with many structures, including the handsome dry stone wall, the brick wall with arch gateway and the pergola and pavilion made in green oak. A high quality *Alitex* glasshouse houses more tender plants. As well as reflecting Geoff Hamilton's style and colour schemes, the garden also illustrates HDRA's concern for the environment in landscape construction. Not all the environmental features are immediately evident. The roof tiles of the pavilion (and vegetable plot edging) are made of recycled polystyrene. Rainwater is collected from this roof and recycled into the wishing well at the centre of the garden. Compost bins in the corner recycle garden waste.

Through the gated arch you reach the country garden, informal in contrast, with wildflower meadow and 'natural' pond, lined with clay.

This garden merges gently into the natural vegetation beyond the plot, connecting the garden to the wider countryside. The bridge and platform are made of green oak with supports made from recycled polystyrene to prevent rotting.

All the gates in the garden were donated by Linda Hamilton, most of them originally having been made for the gardens at Barnsdale.

Look for plants in here named after Geoff Hamilton, a rose, a sweet pea and a Penstemon.

Ryton Garden 16

As you leave the Paradise Garden, turn immediately left and cross over to the **Ryton Garden**. We have created this medium-sized family garden to show how organic methods are applicable to lawns and flower beds, as well as in the vegetable and fruit plot.

The garden is divided by a 'living fence' of espalier trained apple trees planted in 1985. This provides fruit as well as an attractive screen. The vegetables are grown on a bed system with woodchip mulch paths between. Strawberries grow in the border beside the greenhouse, and swap places with the adjoining plantings every three years.

The greenhouse provides the right conditions for cucumber and tomato plants in summer. In winter it houses salad crops and flowering plants. The Black Hamburg vine was planted in 1988 and produces wonderful crops of dessert grapes every autumn.

More fruit is grown in the cage which protects gooseberries, blackcurrants and raspberries from hungry birds. The roof netting is removed in winter to allow the birds in to help with pest control.

The north-facing border is planted with shade-tolerant species that flourish on this cooler, darker side of the garden.

The waste material produced in this garden is returned to the soil to maintain a good structure and provide plants with the necessary nutrients. All weeds and crop wastes are composted; woody prunings are saved for shredding, then either used as a mulch or added to the compost heap. As there is only one mature tree here, autumn leaves are brought in and stacked to make leafmould.

17 Conservation Area

Exit the Ryton Garden by the gate next to the compost bins. Ahead lies the **Conservation Area**. With so much land being lost to roads, building and intensive agriculture, 'wild' areas in gardens are important for the survival of many species.

Much of the conservation area is clothed with trees and shrubs but over to the right is an open area where we have planted a spring flowering meadow.

Cowslips are among the first flowers to appear, followed by a rich diversity of other species, many of which have sown themselves. The meadow is cut in August after the flowers have set seed, and all the hay removed.

The surrounding woodland area has been planted with native species. Larger trees include ash and oak; smaller trees around the edges of the woodland are maple, rowan, wild cherry and alder. Shrubs have been chosen to grow underneath without competition, including species of hazel, hawthorn, holly, spindle and dogwood. All of these, large and small, provide food and shelter for birds, insects and small mammals.

The lake was excavated in 1985. It is an important habitat for many creatures, such as frogs, newts, and damselflies and also has a vital water purification function as part of the **Reedbed Sewage System**.

18 Reedbed Sewage System

All the sewage and waste water on site is collected in underground tanks. Liquids are pumped into a filtering stack above ground. The outflow passes through the main reedbed, which is planted up with specially selected species of reed that are able to clean up the sewage via bacteria living on their roots.

From there it flows into the lake, and then runs into a ditch through the willow coppice.

Up to a third of the willows are cut down to the ground annually to provide a useful source of 'rods' for garden structures, the remainder shredded as mulch. These trees will absorb much of the moisture and any remaining nutrients. By the time any outflow leaves the site, it carries no risk of pollution. Some of the coppiced logs have been piled around the edge of the lake and covered with dry grasses. This provides an ideal habitat for snakes and many insects.

Craftsman's Trees 19

Before the introduction of synthetic materials, different types of timber were widely valued for their individual qualities. **Craftsman's Trees** contains twenty-one species that have had important uses in the past.

The trees were planted into rough pasture in winter 1985/86, each one sponsored by an HDRA member. In the floods and gales of autumn 2000, these trees suffered badly. The *Robinia* started to lean badly and has been braced, whilst a walnut was completely blown over but has resprouted. Many of the specimens will take a hundred years or more to reach their full height.

HDRA Members get free organic advice. For more information pick up a leaflet in the shop.

Uses for some of the trees growing here:

- *Oak – construction, ship-building, furniture*
- *Ash – tools*
- *Holly – mathematical instruments, furniture*
- *Yew – bows, musical instruments.*

Woodland Walk 20

Leading out of this area, we have created an optional **Woodland Walk**, which follows the line of the boundary as far as the soft fruit display. It is planned to plant this with bulbs.

21 RSPB Wildlife Garden

Continuing with the wildlife and conservation theme, HDRA has joined forces with the RSPB to create the **RSPB Wildlife Garden**. Designed by Professor Chris Baines, it includes a rich mixture of diverse habitats. In spring and summer you will see a mini wildflower 'meadow' growing in the middle of the lawn.

The hedge of mixed native species provides food and shelter for a wide range of birds and insects throughout the year. Ledges on the fence behind climbers encourage nesting. The border in front of the hedge is planted with flowers to attract butterflies and moths.

The dry stone wall makes a useful bench, but also extends the range of habitats available for both plants and animals. Ivy-leaved toadflax and thrift have both found homes here.

In summer, a colourful patch of annual flowers beside the gate attracts many beneficial insects. Alyssum, poached egg plant, Californian poppy and sunflowers all flourish.

A marshy area has been created beside the pond for moisture-loving plants such as meadowsweet, purple loosestrife and teasel.

Copies of the HDRA/Search Press book, 'The Small Ecological Garden' are available in the shop.

Rose Garden 22

From the RSPB Wildlife Garden, walk round to the front of the Ryton Garden, and then under the wisteria-festooned grey pergola, which has been made from recycled polystyrene, to the **Rose Garden**. This formal rose garden is a delight to the senses when in full bloom in late July, but what marks it out from many other conventional rose gardens is that fungicides are never used. All rose varieties here have been selected for their ability to resist common problems such as black spot or mildew. Resistance tends to vary with geographical location, and to decline as plants become older.

The roses are mulched in early summer to retain moisture and control weeds. The remains of this mulch are raked off in autumn to expose soil-living pests to their natural enemies, and to remove any fallen rose leaves infected with disease.

23 Sun Clock

As you leave the rose garden, turn left, walking onto an expanse of lawn. Here you will find our **Sun Clock**. By standing on the paved area, with your feet placed on the appropriate month, you become the gnomon of a sundial (always assuming the sun is shining!), and can read off the time from the figures set into the turf. There are two sets of figures – one for Greenwich Mean Time, the other for British Summer Time. The sun clock is accurate to about ten minutes.

HDRA has a factsheet listing the names of resistant rose varieties

24 Mount

Excavating the foundations for The Vegetable Kingdom, resulted in a large quantity of surplus soil. Rather than have it taken off-site we have decided to create a **Mount**. When stabilised and completed, it will provide an excellent view of the gardens. Mounts were standard features of Tudor gardens, remaining fashionable until the 18th century. A number still exist, including one at Cranborne Manor in Dorset, and another at New College, Oxford.

25 Flowers for Pleasure

After viewing the Mount, return to the main path. The garden bounded by a holly and beech hedge has been planted with a colourful and exciting demonstration of spring bulbs, followed by attractive hardy and half hardy annual flowers. For the price of a few packets of seed, you can have a long period of colour in the garden and, in some cases, delightful scent, so they are well worth the little effort needed. Many of these are excellent for attracting beneficial insects into the garden to feed on pests such as aphids. We have also included a range of everlasting flowers for drying as winter decoration.

Calamagrostis Karl Föester looking resplendent after a hard frost.

Diversity in Landscape 26

At the herb garden, the serpentine path to the right of the small cedar greenhouse snakes through the **Diversity in Landscape** display. You enter by way of a large drift of trees and shrubs which make up a demonstration of plants used in large scale plantings for landscape and municipal parks, where ease of maintenance, quick establishment, and ground cover for weed control are essential. The selection of plants on such sites is usually rather limited, so here we are showing some good plants for such situations that are rarely chosen.

Next is a large planting of herbaceous perennials. This is derived from an original idea developed at Weihenstephan in Germany to reduce the need for regular chemical weed control, whilst creating beautiful drifts of flowering perennials with a long season of colour and interest. You will notice grasses planted amongst the other perennials, which add variety of height and texture. This display was created in spring 1997, and has matured nicely. It looks especially striking in winter when the grasses are white with frost.

27 Cook's Garden

You have almost come to the end of your tour, with just four gardens left to see. Emerging from Diversity in Landscape, the garden ahead of you is especially for cooks. The **Cook's Garden** is not quite a kitchen garden or a potager but part of every plant in it is edible, even though there are no common fruits or vegetables. This garden was sponsored by *The Mail on Sunday's* YOU Magazine.

The plants in this garden have been chosen to enhance dishes and complement the standard selection of fruit and vegetables. It is a garden for the enthusiastic cook, looking for the unusual in taste, appearance or texture to allow creativity in the kitchen. It is no coincidence that it is sited next to our famous organic restaurant so that the chef can pop out and pick herbs and delicacies for his menus!

Although the theme for the garden is unusual edibles, the plot is designed to be attractive and ornamental. As you walk along the winding brick path note the mosaic made by former Deputy Head Gardener and designer of the garden, Kathleen Askew. A little further along an Alton octagonal greenhouse shelters tender herbs and winter crops. At the far end of the garden look out for the formal pond with a flow-form water feature powered by a solar panel on the roof behind the fence.

Interesting edible plants in the garden include:

- *Salmonberry (Rubus spectabilis)*
- *Babbington leek (Allium babbingtonii)*
- *Japanese Raisin Tree (Hovenia dulcis)*
- *Kiwi fruit (Actinidia chinensis)*
- *Madeira vine (Anredera cordifolia)*
- *Passion flower (Passiflora edulia) - see below*
- *Red leaved plantain (Plantago major 'Rubrifolia')*
- *Wild ginger (Asarum caudatum)*

Thrive Ryton Gardens Project 28

Next to the Cook's Garden is the **Thrive Ryton Gardens Project**, which is a collaboration between HDRA and Thrive, a separate charity that aims to promote gardening for people with disabilities and other special needs.

The raised beds show examples of various construction methods. The different heights make them suitable for children and adults with a range of abilities: sitting, standing or access from a wheelchair. The paving has changes in texture, helpful to people with a visual impairment for orientation. Also helpful is the use of strongly scented plants in prominent locations to act as aromatic 'landmarks'. The greenhouse has double, sliding doors and no sill to allow easy access for wheelchair users. There is an automatic venting system for temperature control.

The fenced area beside the garden is not open to the public; it is used as a workshop/teaching area for students, practitioners, volunteers and garden users.

29 Memorial Garden

At the far end of the Thrive garden, there is a small **Memorial Garden** dedicated to the memory of Lawrence D. Hills, the founder of HDRA, and his wife Cherry.

Before his death in 1990, Lawrence Hills raised funds for a garden attractive to anyone with a visual impairment. This garden, completed after his death, is the fulfilment of his wishes. All the plants here meet one or more of the following criteria: scented flowers, aromatic foliage, brightly coloured flowers or foliage and interesting texture.

The garden was designed by John Grenside. It is surrounded by high fences to enclose the delicious scents and reduce wind. A wall at approximately waist height makes a useful guide for anyone who can't see well. It forms the edge of a raised area that brings plants up to a convenient height for touching and smelling. The small fountain at the entrance to the garden contains large pebbles, which accentuate the sound of falling water and provide an audible landmark.

Spring bulbs growing in one of the many raised beds in the Thrive Garden.

30 Children's Garden

You reach the **Children's Garden** through the Thrive garden via a gate halfway along the fence to your left. Designed by Jackie Moynihan, the garden aims to educate and entertain children. It is not a play area with

swings and slides but a true garden with fun features such as a willow dome, a 'Swiss chalet' style playhouse, and a turf bench and table. Some bushes have also been planted with the aim of making them into child-oriented topiary sculptures. The educational elements include the plants themselves, the pond and the triangular bed of herbs in the centre.

The garden is available during the week for booking by school parties. A room adjacent to the garden allows indoor activities for such groups. *Please note that adults bringing children into this garden are responsible for the children in their care at all times. We have taken steps to ensure that all of the displays are safe, but HDRA cannot be held responsible for the safety of children on our site.*

That completes your tour of the garden. Retrace your steps to the Thrive garden and then follow the paved path that runs alongside the Diversity in Landscape display, passing the Conference Centre on your right. *Please note that it is not possible to enter the outdoor seating area of the restaurant from this path.*

You are now back at the pergola entrance to the gardens, which you leave via the shop. From here you can also take advantage of refreshments in our new coffee shop, or make use of the restaurant and other facilities.

Coffee Shop

Newly built in 2003, the orangery coffee shop is the place to linger over a delicious cup of organic cappuccino or latté. Fresh cakes, home-made in our restaurant, are an added temptation. Additional seating is available on the terrace.

Ryton Organic Gardens Restaurant

The restaurant at Ryton has become justly famous for the quality of its food. Organic ingredients are used in all dishes, which are prepared fresh daily. Our aim is to provide tasty, nutritious dishes at a reasonable price. Main meals are served between 11am and 3pm, whilst it is possible to get snacks throughout the day. The restaurant is also available for private functions, such as anniversary parties and wedding receptions.

Ryton Organic Gardens Shop

The shop at Ryton underwent a major refurbishment in 2003 and now stocks one of the finest ranges of organic food in the UK. Our policy is to support local organic producers wherever possible, and many of the vegetables on sale are grown here at Ryton. We also have an excellent range of organic wines.

The garden product section of the shop has also been considerably enlarged, specialising in items, such as biological controls, that are not readily found in most garden centres. As you might expect, we stock a wide variety of vegetable seeds, whilst outside there is a plant sales area devoted to herbs, vegetable plants and herbaceous perennials.

Elsewhere in the shop you can find a good gardening book display and a wide choice of gifts.

Heritage Seed Library

HDRA's Heritage Seed Library (HSL) is a collection of 800 rare and unusual vegetable varieties. Many of these have been handed down from generation to generation.

Others are commercial favourites that are no longer sold.

As a member you can get six free packs of HSL seeds each year chosen from a comprehensive catalogue. You will also get a quarterly copy of *Seed News*, a magazine full of fascinating stories and information, plus practical tips on home seed-saving.

For more information and membership subscription rates, pick up a leaflet in the shop, visit our website at **www.hdra.org.uk**, or telephone *024 7630 3517*.

HDRA – the organic organisation

HDRA is an internationally respected organic organisation that researches, demonstrates and promotes organic gardening, farming and food.

HDRA members get these benefits:

- Unlimited free entry to HDRA's gardens at Ryton, near Coventry, Warwickshire, Yalding, near Maidstone, Kent; and all the grounds, including the organic kitchen garden, at English Heritage's Audley End House, near Saffron Walden, Essex.
- Free entry*, by special arrangement with the garden owners to – RHS Wisley in Surrey; RHS Hyde Hall, Essex; RHS Rosemoor, Devon; RHS Harlow Carr, Yorkshire; West Dean Gardens, Sussex; Brogdale, Kent; Barnsdale, Leicestershire; Birmingham Botanical Gardens; Normanby Hall, Lincolnshire, and The Organic Centre, Co. Leitrim, Ireland.
- Free advice from HDRA's experts
- The Organic Way – a full colour, magazine sent four times a year
- 10% discount off all items in 'The Organic Gardening Catalogue'**
- Half price membership of the Heritage Seed Library

Further details on joining are available at reception.

* Applies to one member only, whatever the category of membership
** By special arrangement with Chase Organics

Acknowledgements

Fundraising

We are indebted to the following organisations whose generous support has made The Vegetable Kingdom possible. This list also includes in-kind donors. Our sincere thanks also goes to our many members and other individuals who have contributed financially to this project.

Major Funders

Supported by the **Heritage Lottery Fund**
European Regional Development Fund

Charitable Trusts

Hartnett Trust
Hanson Environment Fund
Lillian Goldman Charitable Trust
Sheepdrove Trust
Underwood Trust
Westminster Foundation

Sponsors

Alitex Ltd *(Tel. 01730 826900)*
Stonemarket Ltd *(Tel. 024 7651 8700)*
Kitchen Garden Magazine *(Tel. 01780 470097)*
Forest Garden plc *(Tel. 01299 251725)*
Organico *(Tel. 0118 951 0518)*
H Chairworks Ltd *(Tel. 0208 247 3700)*
Bramhall Woodware *(Tel. 0114 275 2490)*
Severn Waste Services *(Tel. 01386 443376)*
Becker Underwood *(Tel. 01903 732323)*
Bora *(www.marchioro.it)*
Link-a-Bord *(Tel. 01773 590566)*
Plastic Reclamation Ltd *(Tel. 01744 810001)*
Emmerson Press *(Tel. 01926 854400)*
L C Solutions *(Tel. 01525 279555)*
Forbo-Nairn *(Tel. 01592 643777)*
Bonterra Wines *(Tel. 0207323 5316)*
Andrew Crace *(Tel. 01279 842685)*

Creative Input

The original concept for The Vegetable Kingdom came from Jackie Gear, HDRA's Executive Director, who has been the driving force behind all aspects of the content and design.

The building was designed by Dennis Swain and Paul Leonard of HB Architects, Rugby, and built by Stepnells Ltd, also of Rugby.

Will Daykin and Claire Greswell of Blue – the Design Company were responsible for the indoor display, in conjunction with Jon Hall of HRA. Much of the research was done by HDRA staff, including Pauline Pears, Rebecca Potts and Patsy Dyer. Angela Rawson provided many of the illustrations. We are grateful to Tessa Traeger for providing some of the photographs.

The computer animation was a collaboration between HDRA's webmaster, Simon Levermore, and Robbie Butler. Outside, Isabelle van Groeningen and Gabriella Pape of Land Art Ltd provided the design for Vegetable Inspirations and the Vegetable Way, whilst Bob Sherman, HDRA's Director of Gardens and Gardening, and David Whitehead, Gardens Manager, had overall responsibility for the planting, in conjunction with landscaping contractors, Blakedown Ltd. The Children's Garden was designed by Jackie Moynihan *(Tel. 01328 878851)*.

Written by: Alan and Jackie Gear
Designed by: Rachel Hamdi/Holly Mann
Photographs by: Alan Gear, Dave Lawson, Victoria Albuquerque, Matt White
Executive Production by: Jackie Gear
Printed by: Emmerson Press
Registered Charity no 298104